PHOTOGRAPH: PAUL SPICER

1963 to 2012

In loving memory of Simon Owen

"My mind is now so full of images
that it has run out of room for words."

Simon Owen

RACING
COLOURS

SIMON OWEN

VELOCE PUBLISHING
THE PUBLISHER OF FINE AUTOMOTIVE BOOKS

■ WITH CONTRIBUTIONS FROM ■

CHRIS AMON ■ MARIO ANDRETTI ■ RICHARD
ATTWOOD ■ JEAN BEHRA ■ GIOTTO BIZZARRINI
MARTIN BRUNDLE ■ COLIN CHAPMAN ■ JIM CLARK
JABBY CROMBAC ■ CHUCK DAIGH ■ MICHAEL
DELANEY ■ MARK DONOHUE ■ RENÉ DREYFUS ■ VIC
ELFORD ■ HOWDEN GANLEY ■ FRANK GARDNER
KEN GREGORY ■ JEAN GUICHET ■ FRANÇOIS GUITER
DAN GURNEY ■ JIM HALL ■ CHARLIE HAYES ■ GRAHAM
HILL ■ PHIL HILL ■ DENNY HULME ■ JACKY ICKX
INNES IRELAND ■ DENIS JENKINSON ■ NIKI LAUDA
GUY LIGIER ■ RAYMOND MAYS ■ DENISE McCLUGGAGE
ALAIN MENU ■ JEAN-CLAUD MIGEOT ■ JOHN MILES
STIRLING MOSS ■ GORDON MURRAY ■ JACKIE OLIVER
JO RAMIREZ ■ BRIAN REDMAN ■ ANTOINE DE SAINT-
EXUPÉRY ■ ROY SALVADORI ■ SERGE SAULNIER
CAROL SHELBY ■ JACKIE STEWART ■ JOHN SURTEES
JACQUES SWATERS ■ GILLES VILLENEUVE ■ ROB
WALKER ■ TOM WALKINSHAW ■ DAVID YORKE

www.veloce.co.uk

First published September 2014 by Veloce Publishing Limited, Veloce House, Parkway Farm Business
Park, Middle Farm Way, Poundbury, Dorchester DT1 3AR, England.
This paperback edition first published January 2018
Tel 01305 260068 / Fax 01305 250479 / e-mail info@veloce.co.uk / web www.veloce.co.uk
or www.velocebooks.com.

ISBN: 978-1-787111-94-3 UPC: 6-36847-01194-9
© 2014 & 2018 Simon Owen and Veloce Publishing.

British Library Cataloguing in Publication Data – A catalogue record for this book is available from the British
Library. Typesetting, design and page make-up all by Veloce Publishing Ltd. Printed in India by Replika Press.

FOREWORD

I suppose it was inevitable that my son, Simon, would become interested in motor racing. Motor sport was something I was always interested in, loved watching and reading about; the motor magazines of the day always around the home. Simon was also an easy excuse for the Scalextric motor racing set that I bought and extended. Many Grand Prix events were held on the long table in the spare room. Needless to say my Graham Hill BRM was always beaten by Simon's immaculately turned out Jim Clark Lotus. Perhaps it isn't surprising that Simon was creative, as his dad painted in his spare time, working too as an advertising art director. I am happy to say that there was no disagreement between us about the work we produced, as each admired what the other was doing. Ever since Simon began to follow his heart and produce his first car watercolours we had discussed his work. Simon was always keen and interested to have my views, my approval. Lots of talk about future paintings and compositions, exciting stuff for a dad to be involved in, very lucky too.

It is interesting now to look back at some of his early car paintings and compare them with those painted a few years later. His first were generally of a racing car with large background of team pits or parts of a particular racing circuit. Later, Simon's painting concentrated more closely on the car itself until, finally, he zoomed in, as it were, and took it as far as he could, and yet, retaining all the information, all the excitement that we associate with these wonderful machines. It was obvious, even then, to see how they would eventually morph into the beautiful images that are now reproduced on the following pages. What staggers me, though, is the fact that his usual medium of watercolour was abandoned. A new look demanded a new contemporary medium so all the images contained within this book have been produced entirely upon Simon's Apple Mac computer. That's what I call progress!

David E Owen, 2012

CONTENTS

ACKNOWLEDGEMENTS

When I started out on this great adventure I had little idea what to expect. I certainly had no idea as to the amount of people upon whose cooperation and generosity I would come to depend if I were to see the project through. It is with great pleasure that I can truly say that every single person with whom I had contact with regard to the book, and every publishing company whose authorisation was required to be able to reproduce the quotes used alongside my images, could not have been kinder, more helpful, nor more supportive. It is therefore with great humility and appreciation that I express my gratitude to them all.

And thanks, of course, to Jude, whose scowl every time I hijacked her computer to surf the 'net hid, I'm convinced, deep love and affection! There's so much I couldn't have done, and would never have discovered, without her. She's one of a kind.

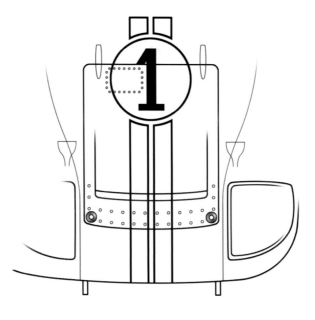

INTRODUCTION

This book is a life's work in some respects, for it draws upon influences and observations gathered from a very early age.

As a kid growing up in the 1960s, my eyes were stimulated by all that was bold, colourful and dynamic, as is the way with kids, but in a way that stood out to me. I remember watching greyhounds racing and being far more interested in the colourful racing 'coats' they wore than the event itself, particularly the red No 6 on a blue and white horizontally striped background. I liked heraldic shields, Napoleonic uniforms, football kits, flags, Belisha beacons and, of course, the bold colours and numbers that dominated the racing cars of the era. You could say that this is a book that has been coming for some time!

In many respects it is a book unlike many others. It is an individual, as all good books should be. It is quirky, eclectic, eccentric even, but in a world intent on reproducing that which has already been regurgitated I personally felt the need for something a bit more idiosyncratic, I can only hope that you agree!

In the modern age it seems that the governing body sees racing numbers on racing cars as somewhat vulgar, too indicative of the competitive sport as opposed to enhancing the corporate business identity. Sponsors want to be associated with money and class, not blood, sweat, oil and tears. Numbers also identify a driver more than they do a team and were therefore seen as an unnecessary indulgence towards the employee behind the wheel. But look at drivers' caps, merchandise, those things that are designed for the fans not the paddock hospitality suits, and numbers come back to the fore. American racing acknowledges its fans more openly than Formula One – and look at their racing numbers – in NASCAR they generally cover both doors and the roof!

Although every image in the book was created on a computer, I made a conscious decision not to turn it into a 'Computer Art' book, resplendent with computer 'grunge' and dramatic mood. Whilst I do appreciate and admire much computer art of that ilk, I felt that it would merely distract from the cars themselves; from the purity of their line and composition, also from the racing colours of a non-grunge era when the large part of these cars were doing their damnedest to cheat the wind.

This is a book that sets out to celebrate the graphic quality and purity of line of these cars. It isn't your orthodox automotive publication. You could say it doesn't know what it's trying to be. But that's the point, it's not trying to be anything, it just is. It is simply the reflection of personal perceptions, of one person's mind, and, in a world intent on globalization, common denominators and format formulae, I hope you will find relief from such limitations in *Racing Colours*.

As an artist I've always believed that one should be able to make a composition out of anything. Whether it be the corner of a room, a brick wall or … a racing car. This book has been created with that belief firmly in mind and, to that end, artistic licence has, in fact, been kept to an absolute minimum. There is always great beauty to be found, as long as you take the time to look for it.

Alongside the hard-edged dynamics of the images, the quotes balance the very graphic nature of the 'panels,' and reflect the deep humanity that permeates beneath the surface of this most cutthroat and technical of sports. On occasion the quotes also touch on just how high the price could often be for those seduced by the sheer exhilaration that these pure racing machines could induce in their pilots.

I leave the last words to the man whose words also accompany the very first of these 'panels,' the French aviator and writer of *Le Petit Prince*, Antoine de Saint-Exupéry. One can only hope that the powers-that-be, both in motor racing and the world as a whole, will ponder them from time to time …

"That man who struggles
in the unique hope of material gain
will harvest nothing worthwhile."

SIMON OWEN
4 November 2011

THE PANELS

"The painting of letters, yet another of those jobs
sacrificed on the altar of progress and profit."

Christian Courtel
in *Les Chiffres à la lettre* (11/02/09), p62 AUTOhebdo

"We take no heed to ask ourselves why we race,
the race itself is more important than the object."

Antoine de Saint-Exupéry

Panhard-Levassor GP
Henri Farman
French GP 1908

"No doubt if I suggest that driving a car at high speed is an art, along with music, painting and literature, I should be greeted by some very cutting remarks from students of the accepted arts; but I really do consider fast driving as an art, an essentially twentieth-century art, and one demanding as much theoretical study, natural flair, learning and practice as any of the classical arts."

Denis Jenkinson

Alfa 40-60hp
Alfredo Conter
Parma-Berceto 1919

"Those who knew him said that Harry Miller was a man who would gamble his last dollar on the drawing board. Naturally, the first worthwhile [American] racing car design was his brainchild. That he designed and constructed such a project in the gloomy fall of 1931 proves that he was in thrall to the passion of the machine, for the creditors were swarming around."

Griffith Borgeson

Miller V16
Shorty Cantlon
Indianapolis 500 1931

"Benoist was the oldest member of the team. He was the team's foundation. Its solid rock. He was still a good driver, if not as quick as he used to be. He had the most striking face, the profile of an eagle, with sharp features, piercing eyes. Through his face you could see something beautiful, his honesty, his class. He was a true chevalier. I liked him a lot."

René Dreyfus

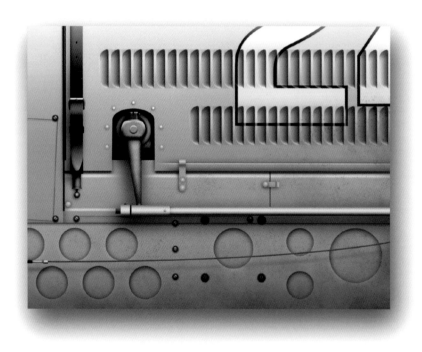

Bugatti Type 59
Robert Benoist
GP de l'ACF 1935

"Briggs Cunningham was a noble anachronism. He loved competition in the truest sense of the term. It was medieval almost, like knights going around looking for other knights to compete with in an honourable fashion. He was a dear man, the purest person I ever knew. For him everything was about the sport."

Denise McCluggage

Cunningham C4RK
Charles Moran & Gordon Bennett
Le Mans 1953

"Only those who do not move, do not die; but are they not already dead?"

Jean Behra

Gordini T24S
Jean Behra
Carrera Panamericana 1953

"Piero Taruffi was an example of a particularly intelligent man in motor racing. He was never in the very first rank, but he certainly did do a great deal of motor racing. Most people watching motor-racing don't appreciate Taruffi's kind of intelligence. I think it's splendid that he finally won the Mille Miglia. Imagine, he ran that race thirteen times. It was a great achievement – he ran alone, you know, I'm sure he knew the roads blindfolded – and he deserved to win."

Stirling Moss

Lancia D24
Piero Taruffi
Tour of Sicily 1954

"We put together full reconnaissance laps in a mixture of cars, Gullwing 300SLRs, 220 saloons and then the first hack 300SLR, Jenks compiling his course notes all the time. On one lap I hit a sheep and telephoned Neubauer who asked, 'Were the other people hurt?' I said, 'There weren't any other people involved. I only hit a sheep …' And he roared 'Ohhh – I thought you said you'd hit a jeep!'"

Stirling Moss

© *Motor Sport* magazine.

Mercedes 300SLR
Stirling Moss & Denis Jenkinson
Mille Miglia 1955

"It was a passion rather than a business: each sale required enormous patience and a number of trips to Italy. And when a client finally said yes, it was a great relief, almost a victory. In the early days the habitual clientele formed a kind of small family. Whenever the owner wanted to acquire a new model I'd take the old one off his hands. Sometimes I'd like to have kept them for myself, as some of the world's most beautiful cars passed through my hands, but at that time I'm afraid that it was impossible for me from a financial point of view."

Jacques Swaters

© *Ecurie Francorhamps* by Gianni Rogliatti, 1992.

Ferrari 500TRC
Lucien Bianchi & George Harris
Le Mans 1957

"Masten Gregory had been driving a Maserati 450S for 'Temple and Buell.' Fangio was going to drive it in Cuba when he got kidnapped. Carroll Shelby was a friend of Temple's, and they shipped it to the Dallas dealership and it sat there in the warehouse six months or so just getting old, which surprised me as it was about as modern a sports-racing car as there was. Having enquired and enquired about it, I finally made an offer and bought it from Temple. I made a pretty low offer, because when we fired it up to check it out it was sitting up on jacks, and it vibrated so bad it fell off! That was how much that engine shuddered."

Jim Hall

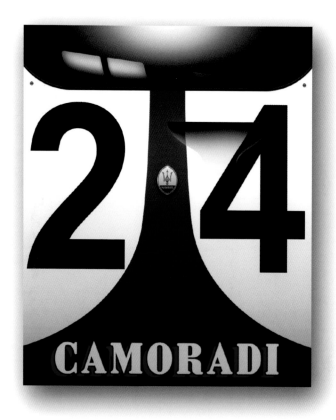

Maserati Birdcage
Masten Gregory & Chuck Daigh
Le Mans 1960

"Stirling and I realized, of course, that the Lotus 18 was a simply fantastic car which conferred an almost insuperable advantage on its driver, and after Goodwood we wanted one very badly. I think that I may have spoken to Colin Chapman in the pits at Goodwood and established that he was as keen for Stirling to drive the car as we were. Colin was longing to win a Grand Prix and he realized that Stirling had a better chance of winning one for him than anyone else, whatever Innes may have thought."

Rob Walker

Lotus 18
Stirling Moss
Monaco GP 1960

"The workmanship of our cars was really nice, but when you looked at the general layout of theirs and how simple everything was, you could see we were out to lunch."

Chuck Daigh

Scarab Type 1
Lance Reventlow
Monaco GP 1960

"I managed a quick start but the Ferraris driven by Stirling and Mike Parkes were just too fast. I had my work cut out driving the Aston Martin. It was a big hairy beast to drive, and on St Mary's, for instance, it would get into a real wallow. You had to hold on tight and generally drag the car round."

Jim Clark

Aston Martin DB4GT Z
Jim Clark
Goodwood TT 1961

"People say I am crazy because I get sideways sometimes. Jesus, let me tell you, a Ferrari driver who didn't get sideways these last five years would not have been a racing driver! You know what, I remember Phil Hill saying that in 1961 he would very happily have swapped some of his horsepower for some of the British cars' handling. Believe me, I know what he meant …"

Gilles Villeneuve

© Nigel Roebuck, *Autosport* magazine.

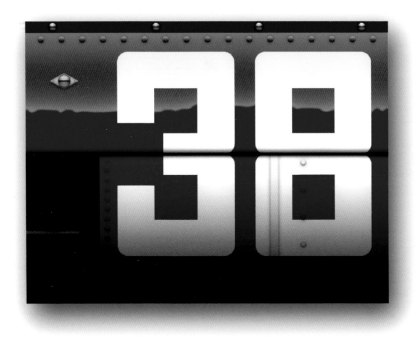

Ferrari 156 V6
Phil Hill
Monaco GP 1961

"I knew we would win when Tavoni hung out a signal saying 'GINTHER GIVE ALL,' but throughout the race Stirling thought that the Ferraris were just playing cat and mouse with him and could have passed him at will; he never really believed he could win until he took the chequered flag. I thought it was Stirling's greatest drive; in fact, I thought it was the greatest drive, by any driver, that I had ever seen in my entire life."

Rob Walker

Lotus 18 (open-sided)
Stirling Moss
Monaco GP 1961

"I might well have gone to Rattlesnake Raceway before that first race for Chaparral. I do remember I did not much like going there, having to tear around this little track that they had all been round 15,000 times and that they knew like the back of their hand. It was like trying to beat one of those Ferrari 'Collaudatore' test drivers at Modena – it just cannot be done."

Phil Hill

Ferrari 250 GTO
Show Car
N/A 1962

"My fondest memory of the GTO is probably the day that I went from England to Maranello to pick up the car. I was with Ronnie Hoare, of Maranello Concessionaires, who had come to collect the car that Mike Parkes was going to drive, and we had the most wonderful journey you could imagine driving back from Maranello to England. I remember roaring through the factory gates and then driving in very close company to Ronnie Hoare and his GTO, we amazed a fair few people on the roads. It was a fantastic journey, and, as the cars were new, we had been told at the factory not to go beyond 5500rpm. But on the roads of the time that was already bloody quick!"

Innes Ireland

© *Auto Passion*, No 74, Hammel Group, 2008.

Ferrari 250 GTO
Innes Ireland
Goodwood TT 1962

"One of the most pleasant memories I have is that the GTO made me feel important in that period. I was a young driver, so when Luigi Chinetti asked me to drive a NART GTO with the NART colours at Bridgehampton it was like a dream come true. The GTO was a jolly good car, one of the most beautiful competition cars I have ever driven. It was always easy to drive fast because you always felt very secure. And then there was the amazing engine noise: a perfect sound."

Charlie Hayes

Ferrari 250 GTO
Bob Grossman & Glenn Roberts
Le Mans 1962

"The 250 GTO arrived in France by lorry, but had kept its Italian plates so as to avoid any questions at Customs. Because of this sordid 'detail,' we couldn't use the car on the road when we weren't racing! Its engine, derived from that of the 250TR, offered both torque and lots of power. Although having better performance than the 250GT SWB, the 250GTO especially offered better road-holding and better braking capabilities. It was nearly perfect and incredibly polyvalent. However, at the 24 Hours, we were still only 'privateers' and, despite the performance and potential of the car, it was out of the question for us to go and tease the 'official' team cars ..."

Jean Guichet

© *Rétroviseur* magazine, No 223, 2007.

Ferrari 250 GTO
Pierra Noblet & Jean Guichet
Le Mans 1962

"The GTO was the only car in which Ferrari was totally involved. He would spend three or four hours a day in my department closely following the development of every little detail. Perhaps it was this almost fatherly rapport between Ferrari and the 250 GTO, which turned it into the amazing car which won so many races and fascinated the motoring world."

Giotto Bizzarrini

Ferrari 250 GTO
Fernand Tavano & Andre Simon
Le Mans 1962

"Mike had everything I thought I wanted – a smart flat in Modena, an airplane, a fast motorbike, a Ferrari, a Bentley, Cooper S and a hot Imp. But he went upstairs, looked wistfully at the children in bed, came down and said 'Good heavens, you have done well, Tim.'"

Tim Fry

Ferrari 250 GTO
Mike Parkes
Goodwood TT 1963

"We took the GT40s to the Le Mans test weekend in April. 'Lucky' Casner was there with the latest Maserati. In Modena, Lucky and I had dinner often, to talk about everything, not just racing cars. He was my friend. At Le Mans we were laughing in the paddock, and a few minutes later the big Maserati went off into the trees at the end of the Mulsanne Straight and he didn't come back."

Jo Ramirez

Maserati Tipo 151/1
'Lucky' Lloyd Casner & Andre Simon
Le Mans 1963

"On Saturday evening I was going through the Mulsanne Kink, which was just about flat in the E, and suddenly I felt the car sliding. Oil. Several people had already gone off, so I was a late comer, so to speak. There were cars up the bank and in the trees, an Alpine was on fire on the other side of the track. I hit the bank with a huge impact, and somehow I was shot out through the E-type's back window onto the road. I was lying on the tarmac drenched in fuel because the tank had ruptured, my car was burning and the flames were coming along the trail of petrol towards me. But I literally couldn't move. Finally I managed to get my fingernails into the grass verge and pulled myself up this little earth mound. That's all I remember."

Roy Salvadori

Jaguar E-type
Roy Salvadori & Briggs Cunningham
Le Mans 1963

"We'd had problems with one engine on the two GTOs entered. Our slower car (4153) lost third to the factory 250P of Parkes and Maglioli, but our faster GTO (4293) finished a strong second. It was a fantastic result and we were all elated. The celebrations continued for most of Sunday night and, after the prizegiving on Monday, we packed and fuelled up the GTOs for the drive home. At about seven in the evening we stopped for something to eat at Rambouillet, south-west of Paris. During dinner I had the crazy idea to call in at the Pigalle district to visit a nightclub to complete the celebrations. So we drove the race-stained GTOs into the centre of Paris at night, parked them in the street and spent a fourth night without sleep. In the morning we fuelled up again and drove back to Brussels."

Jacques Swaters

© *Classic & Sports Car* magazine, January 2001 edition.

Ferrari 250 GTO
'Eldé' & Pierre Dumay
Le Mans 1963

"The Americans were very friendly, but at the same time they were trying everything to screw Team Lotus. In qualifying, for example, there are certain procedures when you line up in the pits – and they made sure Lotus didn't know these procedures properly. So there was a general air of crusade within Team Lotus, and Jimmy was very much part of that."

Jabby Crombac

Lotus 29
Jim Clark
Indianapolis 500 1963

"For all the magic that Jim Clark had, his Achilles heel was that he wasn't too good under pressure, especially from the people that he feared; being as honest as the day is long, he always said that Dan Gurney was the most underrated driver of his generation, and that in a good car Dan was the best he ever raced against."

Jo Ramirez

© *Memories of a Racing Man* by Jo Ramirez, 2005.

Lotus 29
Dan Gurney
Indianapolis 500 1963

"It was a beautifully balanced car, better than the F1 and F2 Coopers as it turned out. It was only when I got out of the car that I realized I must have done quite well, there was a buzz about the place. Indeed, Ken offered me the drive pretty much there and then."

Jackie Stewart

Cooper T72 F3
Jackie Stewart
Goodwood Test 1964

"Innes was loyal to me; not just for the three seasons we raced together, but for the rest of his life. For all the fun and games he had, he was a man of incredibly high principles and he felt crushed by the way he'd been treated by Colin Chapman. In all the years I was in racing, I never met a more loyal man."

Ken Gregory

Ferrari 250 GTO '64
Innes Ireland & Tony Maggs
Le Mans 1964

"The glory of Ferrari was the important thing to Mr Ferrari; much more important than anything else. We had a good relationship but he became a hindrance to the team: he was out of date and the politics got in the way of development. Opportunities went to waste: we could have won two more championships if we'd been able to harness all the resources and materials that were available."

John Surtees

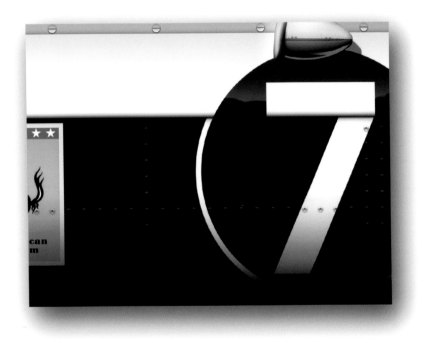

Ferrari 158 V8
John Surtees
USA GP 1964

"Once, standing with Enzo outside his office, he commented on a 250 Lusso parked ahead. 'That car is too beautiful. A Ferrari should look fierce and angry.' The result was the more aggressive 275GTB. His instructions to Bizzarrini for the GTO were probably the same."

John Surtees

Ferrari 250 GTO
Ulf Norinder & 'Pico' Troberg
Targa Florio 1964

"Hap got the fastest qualifying lap at Laguna Seca in the 2C by standing in the pits. We were qualifying and I was talking to him about it in the pits and we were discussing about what to do where, what gear where, and so forth. And he said, 'OK,' put on his helmet and he put his leg over the car to go out in it for the first time and was just sitting down when they came over the loudspeakers saying, 'Hap Sharp has just set a new lap record.' So he got back out of the car! We never did quite work that one out ..."

Jim Hall

Chaparral 2C
Jim Hall
Riverside 500 1965

"It was a big-budget operation, a great setup, and the [Cobra Daytonas] were wonderful to drive. I just loved them, and we were well ahead of the GTO Ferraris in our class at Le Mans. You drove them much like the 250F – all traction."

Chris Amon

Shelby Cobra Daytona
Dan Gurney & Jerry Grant
Le Mans 1965

"Those big stockers weighed nearly two tons, they'd run 160mph down the back straight, and they had drum brakes. If changing direction in an F1 car is like a water-bug darting across the surface of a pond, driving a NASCAR sedan on a road circuit is like trying to dock an aircraft carrier."

Dan Gurney

Motor Sport magazine.

Ford Galaxie
Dan Gurney
Riverside 500 1965

"Siffert was incredibly single-minded. I remember one occasion when Brian Redman came in to hand over to him earlier than expected. Seppi wasn't even in the pit, but somewhere out the back. When he saw what was happening he ran to the back of the pit to jump over the counter, caught his foot on it, and went sprawling on the road. His overalls were ripped, and his knees torn to pieces, but he never gave them a glance. Hurled himself into the cockpit, and was gone! Amazing bloke …"

David Yorke

Maserati Tipo 65
Jo Siffert & Jochen Neerpasch
Le Mans 1965

"I feel very strongly that the ultimate in any activity is of direct value to the country achieving it. It becomes incumbent upon those of us who have the ability to try to produce a car which will securely uphold our place in international competition."

Raymond Mays

BRM P261 V8
Graham Hill
Monaco GP 1965

"Don wanted an American in one of the cars, so the drivers were me and George Follmer. Poor old George hated me. I had the advantage of knowing the circuits and I kept on being quicker than him, and at the end of the year he went back to America.

"So in Can-Am, an arena where he had been champion and knew the circuits, he thought he'd turn the tables on this cheeky little Limey. But he didn't. To be fair, we were pretty evenly matched, but I came out on top."

Jackie Oliver

Lotus 23
George Follmer
Road America 1965

"There's no doubt in my mind that Jimmy won that race. He'd lapped Hill before his first spin and then Graham unlapped himself when Jimmy spun again coming off Turn 4. He didn't pit for tyres either time and we still had like a 40-second lead after his second spin. Chapman had the head of timing and scoring from the RAC in our pit every May and USAC had some little old ladies scoring the race. The lap charts clearly showed Clark was the winner but it didn't matter. He got screwed."

Allan McCall

Lotus 38
Jim Clark
Indianapolis 500 1966

"The top drivers in my era were Jimmy, Jackie and Jochen Rindt. And Jack Brabham: he was a hard old bastard, and he drove some cracking races. He got a bit diverted when he was setting up his own company, but in his last race, Mexico 1970, he came past me and Denny absolutely going for it, on the grass, up the curbs like always: he was 44 years old then."

Chris Amon

Brabham BT19
Jack Brabham
Dutch GP 1966

"We definitely got a jump on the competition in the aerodynamics arena in about 1964. I had built a car that had bad lift characteristics and I wanted to cure that during the winter of '63-64. I managed to do it. Then I thought, 'Well, if I can eliminate lift, why can't I continue right on through zero and go negative? Why don't I push down on this thing and see if I can increase the traction?' And by golly, I was able to do that, too."

Jim Hall

Chaparral 2E
Jim Hall
Leguna Seca 1966

"Rindt and Rodriguez were a good combination. You could rely on Jochen to be right up front. And you could also almost rely on him falling off the road or blowing an engine. Pedro, on the other hand, was dependable, easy on the car, but quick – a future champion, I think."

Roy Salvadori

Cooper T81 – Maserati
Jochen Rindt
French GP 1966

"At first nobody could drive the early GT40s, but we did a tremendous amount of work on them, and eventually they were nice cars. I hate to think how much money Ford spent on winning Le Mans, but they did what they set out to do. I can't remember how many cars they ran at Le Mans in '67, but it was a lot – nine or something."

Frank Gardner

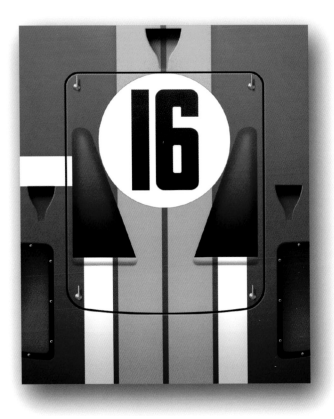

Ford GT40
Frank Gardner & John Whitmore
Le Mans 1966

"We took the lead some time in the morning and only then did we allow ourselves to back off a little. It was a most enjoyable race. The only sad memory I have of it was the staged finish. We didn't benefit from it as we had a comfortable lead by the time the Ford edict went out, but Ken Miles, who shared the other car with Denny Hulme, was very bitter about it, and sadly he was killed just a few weeks later."

Chris Amon

Ford GT40
Chris Amon & Bruce McLaren
Le Mans 1966

"Ken should have won the race, and in most everyone's mind he did win the race. I take full responsibility for it, and I'm very sorry for it because Ken was killed at Riverside two months later. Every time you go racing you put your reputation on the line."

Carroll Shelby

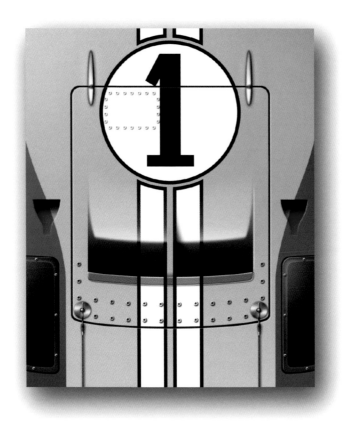

Ford GT40
Ken Miles & 'Denny' Hulme
Le Mans 1966

"There's so much about racing that's real and doesn't have to be dramatised or invented. There's the memorization of the circuit ... driving as far as you can see by the beams of your lights ... the flash in your mirror as the faster car comes by ..."

Steve McQueen

Ford GT40
Richard Holquist, Bruce Jennings & Oscar Kovelski
Sebring 1966

"There was a hairpin at Fuji and I don't think most of the Americans had ever had to deal with one before. At least it didn't seem that way. Qualifying was in their style, one at a time, and the first six or seven just never made it round at all. Graham, Jackie and I sat in the pits, awaiting our turn and getting more and more hysterical. Every time we'd hear an Offenhauser screaming down to the hairpin absolutely flat, then a violent screeching of locked wheels, then a brief silence – then finally BOOF! as they clobbered the bank! A couple of minutes would then elapse before some red-faced American would walk in, scowling at us …"

Chris Amon

© *Forza Amon!* by Eoin Young, 2003.

DO NOT OVERFILL

Lola Ford T90
Jackie Stewart
Fuji Indy 200 1967

"It was quite clear to me that John couldn't possibly do all the things he was trying to do and hope to do any of them well enough to be successful. I thought that in everyone's best interests – especially John's – I had better try and get him out of the seat, so one day I said to him, 'John, you're doing far too much. Why not chuck the driving? You can go on doing the testing so that you know how the car behaves and how to set it up properly, but let someone else do the race driving.' Slightly to my surprise he didn't react too badly to this suggestion, perhaps because under the strain of his fantastic workload he had begun to reach the same conclusion."

Rob Walker

© *Rob Walker* by Michael Cooper-Evans, 1993.

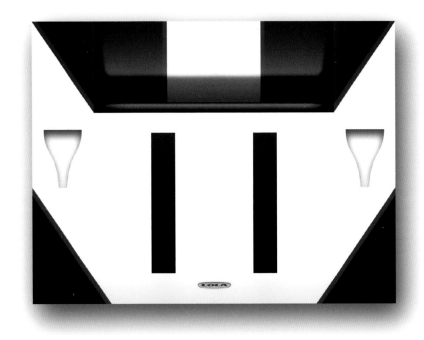

Lola T70
John Surtees & David Hobbs
Le Mans 1967

"Ford attacked the thing pretty well, I can tell you, showed everybody how to spend money. The problem was Ford had this policy that they wanted an American in every car. Fine when it was a Dan Gurney, but some of them were just oval racers, and they'd never raced at night. I was with Roger McCluskey and Denny Hulme was with Lloyd Ruby. It was a shame because if Denny and I could have shared a car we'd have strode right along. Ruby crashed Denny's car around midnight, and then at five in the morning McCluskey walked back into the pits and said he'd had a little accident. Denny said, 'We're on finishing money, we may as well go and see if we can get the bloody thing running.' So we walked down to the Esses and the first thing I saw was this radiator up in the trees. I said, 'I don't think there's going to be much to share with you, Denis.' If that was a little accident I'd hate to see Roger have a big one."

Frank Gardner

Ford GT40 Mk II
Frank Gardner & Roger McCluskey
Le Mans 1967

"Jo Schlesser was a wonderful guy, very funny. He made jokes about everybody and everything, and could take off all the important people in motor sport. He was like the Graham Hill of French motor sport. His death at Rouen in the air-cooled Honda in 1968 should never have happened. That car was totally unsorted and I'm sure he was out of his depth. But as a Frenchman he wanted to drive it in the French Grand Prix."

Richard Attwood

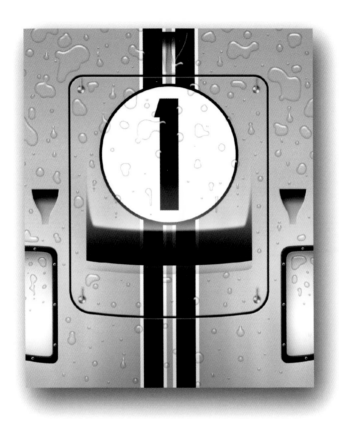

Ford GT40 Mk II
Guy Ligier & Jo Schlesser
1000km de Paris 1967

"Although he was pre-eminent as a racing driver, his most profound influence, certainly on me and all his close associates, was not his ability as a racing driver, but his success as a man. He was so thoroughly adjusted to life and its problems, he had such a thorough integrity of his own that it is very difficult for others to compare themselves in the same street. He was fit, he was honest – 'integrity' is the best single word to describe his qualities. This is the man I shall always remember, not simply a man who won a record number of races. He was a man who set an example to others."

Colin Chapman

© *Jim Clark – Portrait of a Great Racing Driver*
by Graham Gauld, 1968.

Lotus 49
Jim Clark
French GP 1967

"The thing I learned from Bruce, is to do whatever needs doing; no excuses. If you get into a problem, the easy thing to do is say 'Oh, we can fix that tomorrow.' That isn't the way to do it – let's fix it now. Tonight. Even if it means pulling the guttering off the side of the building or cutting up the secretary's desk, you do it. Bruce had that in spades when the chips were down. He was a fantastic leader."

Howden Ganley

McLaren M7A
Bruce McLaren
Mexican GP 1968

"My drive at Monaco in '68 ... it was a good drive, I think, but I felt, on other days, I'd driven better races and got no reward. My all-time favourite track was Clermont-Ferrand, a fantastic circuit if ever there was. But I always liked Monaco – I liked the precision of it all."

Richard Attwood

BRM V12
Richard Attwood
Monaco GP 1968

"Racing throws the truth in your face immediately."

Jean-Claud Migeot

Howmet TX Turbine
Hugh Dibley & Bob Tullius
Le Mans 1968

"Basically, Elf was a technical company run by engineers. They were very good at what they did – deep sea drilling and so on – but they didn't know how to go about marketing their company. We made a big survey and it came up with one answer: motor racing. At the same time, Matra was looking for a way to demonstrate their technical ability. They had already made a Formula 3 and a Formula 2 car. It was obvious for Elf to join Matra. We decided on a 4-year contract, which was very rare at the time. We announced it at the Monte Carlo Rally and said we would win in Formula 3, then in Formula 2, and in the third year win in Formula 1. For the fourth year we would win Le Mans. Everyone laughed."

François Guiter

Matra V12
Jean-Pierre Beltoise
Monaco GP 1968

"Someone once described Graham Hill as the Douglas Bader of motor racing, and that was a pretty perceptive description. He was a folk hero, a sort of national institution."

Rob Walker

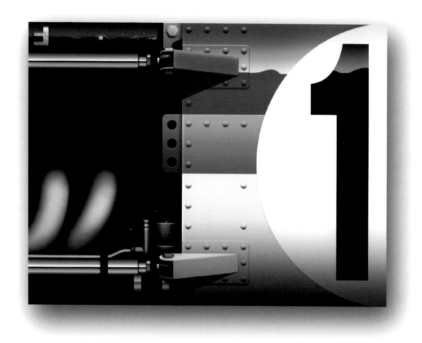

Lotus 49B
Graham Hill
Spanish GP 1968

"The thing about Patrick, was that although sometimes he would do things that drove you mad, it was impossible to stay angry with him for long – he was like a little boy all his life, and that definitely worked in his favour a time or two. He was always wanting to go skiing or motorcycling, things like that, and he had this trusting belief that everything would be alright in the end. More than anyone I've known, he lived for the present."

Ken Tyrrell

Alpine A220
Patrick Depailler & Gérard Larousse
1000km de Paris 1968

"That was the first and only time Porsche used the photo of a driver, not the car, to promote a win. When I talked to Helmet Bott about it afterwards, he said they did it because, for once, it wasn't Porsche that won, it was the driver."

Vic Elford

Porsche 907
Vic Elford & Umberto Maglioli
Targa Florio 1968

"I can't say I was ever personally concerned about my own safety in the car. I'm something of a fatalist – I figure no two accidents are ever quite the same and, even if you're prepared for every contingency, something else is going to get you some day."

Mark Donohue

Sunoco Lola T70
Mark Donohue & Chuck Parsons
Daytona 1969

"A lot of people go through life doing things badly, racing's important to men who do it well. When you're racing, it's life. Anything that happens before or after … it's just waiting."

'Michael Delaney' (Steve McQueen)

© Writer: Harry Kleiner. *Le Mans* film, Cinema Center Films.
A 'Solar' production. Paramount Pictures, 1971.

Porsche 917K
Michael Delaney
Le Mans 1970

"It was a lovely sensation. All I can liken it to is when you're sitting on a runway in a jet and they release the brake and suddenly the noise gets left behind and all you have is the feeling of silent acceleration. At Hethel you could hear the pads rattling in the calipers, the rose joints in the suspension rattling over the seams in the concrete, the tyres – and the wind."

John Miles

Lotus 56B
Emerson Fittipaldi
Italian GP 1971

"If Colin Chapman had known how much effort went into making the 908/3 light, and how light it was, he would've had a fit. But I felt so secure in it that I never considered it unsafe. It was so controllable that the confidence it gave me was huge."

Vic Elford

Porsche 908/3 'Martini'
Helmut Marko & Gijs Van Lennep
Targa Florio 1971

"I enjoyed the life. But I said to my wife: 'So many of my friends are being killed. Most of them don't believe that it will ever be them, but I think it more than likely that I *will* be killed.' So I decided to stop."

Brian Redman

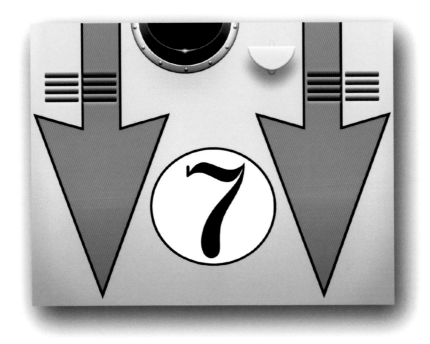

Porsche 908/3 'Gulf'
Brian Redman & Jo Siffert
Targa Florio 1971

"The early 917s had a gas-filled alloy chassis. There was a big gas pressure gauge in the cockpit to keep you informed of the chassis' condition. If it zeroed, they said, that meant the chassis was broken, and I should drive it *mit* care back to the pits. Once I knew what the gauge was for, I also knew that if it zeroed I was not going to drive it *mit* care anywhere. I was going to park the bastard there, and then pick up my deutschmarks and get home to Mum ..."

Frank Gardner

Porsche 917/20
Reinhold Jöst & Willi Kauhsen
Le Mans 1971

"Ron [Dennis] was a brilliant mechanic. Once, in Brazil, Ron did an immaculate job on an engine. A crowd formed and clapped when he finished. He's an artist. He may not have been the easiest person to get on with – his perfectionism is his law – but he's a genius."

Tony Vlassopoulo

© *F1 Racing* magazine. "Ron's First Racing Team" by Marcus Simmons, May 2008.

Rondel Brabham BT36
Graham Hill
Thruxton 1971

"Ron Dennis said that he would never change the name, and he kept his word. I find that absolutely wonderful, but I'd like the new generation to really know who the first 'McLaren' was. Like Enzo Ferrari … people know who Enzo was, and yet we see Team McLaren winning so often without Bruce's image being anywhere in sight."

Denny Hulme

Yardley McLaren M19C
Denny Hulme
South African GP 1972

"I didn't think I stood a chance ... and even quite a long way into the race I still thought the Ferraris were just playing with me."

Stirling Moss

Ferrari 365GTB/4
Mike Parkes, Jean-Louis Lafosse & Jean-Jacques Cochet
Le Mans 1972

"Those were racing cars you could really grow an affection for. It's amazing how much you grow into part of a car when you're in it hour after hour. I've driven Fords and Alfas, but man, to drive a Ferrari sports car ... Well, it's on a level entirely of its own."

Mario Andretti

© *F1 Racing* magazine. "Andretti" by Alan Henry, December 2008.

Ferrari 312PB
Jacky Ickx & Mario Andretti
Brands Hatch 1972

"Ken ran the tightest and most efficient team in the business but, as I arrived in Long Reach, near Ockham, I couldn't believe that the world championship car had been built and run from this place. There were three sheds, three Portakabins, and a muddy yard for a parking place; the whole ensemble was enough to put off a travelling salesman."

Jo Ramirez

Tyrrell 006
Jackie Stewart
German GP 1973

"At the time, before ground-effect cars, the driving style was generally rather tail-out and opposite-lock, sliding through the turns. But not Carlos, he was always very precise and neat and tidy – unspectacular but very fast; the fastest of all on his day … but he persistently suffered these psychological ups and downs."

Gordon Murray

Brabham BT44B
Carlos Reutemann
South African GP 1975

"As a pragmatic Austrian, the whole sense of drama was difficult for me to understand. But I like to think that I was pragmatic enough to play the game they wanted me to. For example, when I first drove the B3 at Fiorano I told Piero Lardi, who was translating for his father Mr Ferrari, that the car was shit. Piero nervously told me that I really should pull my punches. So I said that it had too much understeer, which it did. So Mr Ferrari told me that I had a week in which to lap one second faster round Fiorano, otherwise I was out. So we made the modifications and delivered the result. It was a piece of cake, actually."

Niki Lauda

© *Motor Sport* magazine.

Ferrari 312T
Niki Lauda
Italian GP 1975

"I'm unusual for an engineer in that I went to art school when I was 13. I still do a bit of drawing and painting, and I love styling. I couldn't bring myself to make an ugly car. Before wind tunnels, shaping a car was all practical – wool tufts and intelligent guesses. Even with basic wind tunnel work there were parts of the car that made no difference to performance. So why not make it look nice? Most engineers are not sympathetic to artistic stuff at all; they couldn't draw something pretty if you put a gun to their head."

Gordon Murray

Brabham BT45
Carlos Pace
South African GP 1976

"I don't have any fear of a crash, I never think I can hurt myself. It seems impossible to me. If you believe it can happen to you, how can you possibly do the job properly? If you're never over eight-tenths or whatever, because you're thinking about a shunt, you're not going as quick as you can. And if you're not doing that, you're not a racing driver. Most of the guys in Formula 1 ... well, to me, they're not racing drivers. They're doing half a job, and I can't figure why they do it at all ..."

Gilles Villeneuve

Ferrari 126C2
Gilles Villeneuve
Belgian GP 1982

"When I did Rally GB in 1999, I was testing in Wales, and Sainz and Auriol were in the other two works Toyotas. We were practicing on a special stage, maybe 15 miles long, and by the end of the day, I was within half a second a mile of the other two – and I was bloody impressed with myself! Anyway, we got to the first stage, where it was misty and raining hard – and I was *15 seconds* a mile slower! OK, the other two had done it a few times in earlier years, and this was my first time, but … Jesus! They're talking about 'flat here' and 'flat there' – 120mph over a blind crest in *fog* sort of thing – and I'm thinking, 'I can't see where I'm going …' It was then that I realised those guys have a talent we just don't know about."

Martin Brundle

© *Motor Sport* magazine.

Lancia Delta HF
Miki Biasion
World Rally Championship 1987

"There weren't many people around because it was a private area but I'm so glad I was there. Ayrton Senna was visibly braking eight meters later than anybody else, but it was his car that was amazing. You could hear all the others banging around under braking. But as he braked the whole car just shook. You could hear nothing – except for *phphphphph*. It made an immediate impression on me. Later I heard Ayrton had to come into the pits because he was looking down on himself from above the car. I'm very down-to-earth and if I hadn't seen it, I'd have said, 'Okay, whatever, it was just a fantastic lap.' But now I believe it because I saw it and I heard it. Something definitely happened that Saturday and I believe it was special because I've never seen a racing car do this. Never, ever, ever. It gives me goose pimples to talk about it – and I have no doubt it was the same the whole way round the lap."

Alain Menu

© *Overdrive – Formula 1 in the Zone* by Clyde Brolin, 2010.

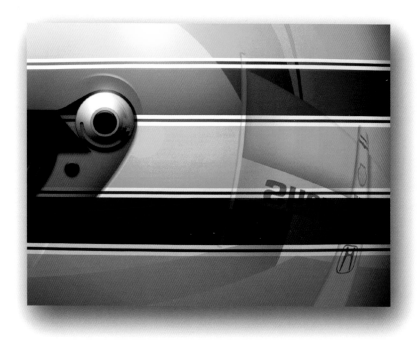

McLaren MP4/4
Aryton Senna
Monaco GP 1988

"I don't think I've seen anything like it in my life. It became so emotional, grown men with tears running down their faces. You could feel the emotion oozing out of everywhere. You could touch it, couldn't you? It was just something which one has never experienced before."

Tom Walkinshaw

Jaguar XJR9LM
Jan Lammers, Johnny Dumfries & Andy Wallace
Le Mans 1988

"My biggest regret was having missed the world title. We could have won it in '79, '80 or '81. With that, the team would still be standing; I'd be Frank Williams."

Guy Ligier

Ligier JS39
Martin Brundle
Japanese GP 1993

"When I had that puncture on Mulsanne in the middle of the night in '99 it was probably the most disappointed I've ever been in my life. I put my heart and soul into that Toyota project so I'd had enough of Le Mans for a little while. It was a car that should have won the race, and didn't."

Martin Brundle

Toyota GT One
Martin Brundle
Le Mans 1999

"We could barely believe our ears on Thursday, at the end of the first part of practice, when McNish recorded the best provisional time of 3'23"650. In the Audi pit they were all shouting 'Yes!', as if they'd won the race, when in actual fact the lap was really nothing special. That's when we realised that they had a problem, because that lap was really nothing special."

Serge Saulnier

Peugeot 908 HDi
David Brabham & Alexander Wurz & Marc Gené
Le Mans 2009

"We are all on this planet for such a short time, aren't we? And my value, your value – among six billion people!" – doesn't change anything, does it? You're in, you're out. But every one of these six billion people has a different story."

Jacky Ickx

THE PROCESS

Although Simon never intended for his process work to be
shown in this book, it has been included in this version.
It gives an amazing insight into his creative and talented mind.
This is the 'essence of Simon,' and all who knew and loved him,
understood and appreciated that.

THE THUMBNAIL SKETCHES

Panhard-Levassor GP

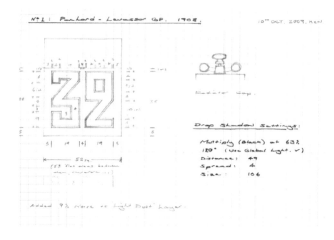

Test Grill (treated)

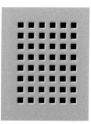

Alfa 40-60hp

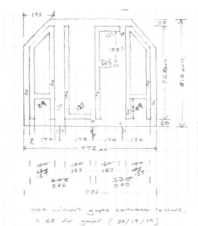

LETTERS TOO THICK: Reduce from 34 to 30.

|38|30|97|30|28|30|127|20|30|127|28|30|97|30|38| =772!

P.S. This all changed somewhat!

(Radiator Grill Horizontals = 20% opacity.)

Miller V16

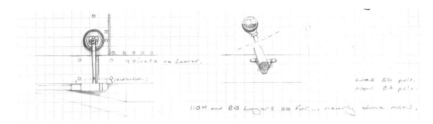

9 Rivets to Louver.

(reduction)

Was 56 pxls.
Now 84 pxls.

110M and 83 Louvers 50 far... nearly done now).

Bugatti Type 59

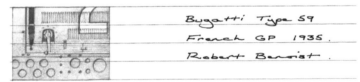

Bugatti Type 59

French GP 1935.

Robert Benoist.

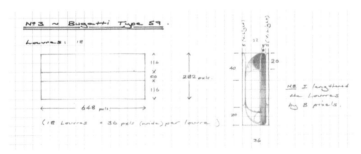

Nº3 ~ Bugatti Type 59.

Louvres: 18

116
X
60
X
116

282 pxls.

648 pxls

(18 Louvres = 36 pxls (wide) per louvre)

40
20

20

36

NB I lengthened
the Louvres
by 8 pixels.

Bugatti louvres

Aston Martin DB4GT Z

Aston Martin DB4GT Zagato.
Goodwood TT 1961.
Jim Clark.

2 VEV

Ferrari 156 V6

So ... back to work! I'll adapt + enlarge the unfinished
Ferrari 156 V6 first and then go back to the beginning.

Nº13 ~ 1961 Ferrari 156 V6   N.E.W.

Top Rivet Spacings:

1294
1158
~15 Rivets @ 22
= 330 pvls.
∴ 828 ÷ by 16 gaps
= 51.75 pvls per gap.

832 ÷ = 1206

1154
~15 Rivets @ 22 (330)
∴ 824 ÷ by 16 gaps
= 51.5 ...

17 Rivets @ 22 = 374
16 Gaps @ 52 = 832
Added = 1206.
∴ 88 pvls for two 'end' gaps
= 44 pixels each.

Lower Rivet Spacings:

44 pvls.

13 Rivets @ 22 = 286 pvls.
14 Gaps (within 162) = 11.57...

10 x 12 = 120   2 x 11 = 22   1x10 = 10
1x9 = 9
8 x 12 = 108   3 x 11 = 33
6 x 12 = 96   3 x 11 = 33   1 x 10 = 10
1x9 = 9   1x8 = 8
1x7 = 7

1 x 11 / 7 x 12 / 3 x 11 / 1 x 10 / 1 x 9 / 1 x 8 / 1x7

1026

Lotus 18

All but Stirling done and already 76 Layers used ...!

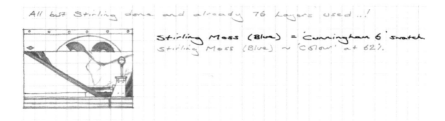

Stirling Moss (Blue) = Cunningham 6 snatch
Stirling Moss (Blue) ~ 'Colour' at 62%.

Ferrari 250 GTO –1964

N° 29 ~ 1964 Ferrari 250 GTO '64.

Width of Numbers: 70 - 74 pxls. The numbers, as usuall, were hand-made

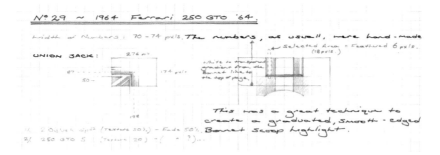

of Selected Area = Feathered 6 pxls.
(18 pxls.)

UNION JACK: 276 n?

87 ....

50 ~   174 pxls

White to transparent
gradient from the
Bonnet line to
the top of page.

This was a great technique to
create a graduated, smooth-edged
Bonnet scoop highlight.

1/ 2 O'clock split (Texture 50%.) - Fade 50%
2/ 250 GTO 5 (Texture 20) ~(" ?)...

Chaparral 2C

NOTE: WHEN IN KEN, WITH THE 'CHAPARRAL' BOOK AT MY
DISPOSAL, CHECK OUT THE CURIOUS 'NACA' DUCT SHAPE AT
THE TOP/RIGHT OF THE DOOR, ONCE IDENTIFIED, ADD TO
THIS PANEL.

This is the shape of
the very half metal latch
recessed into the TOP LEFT... of the door.

Ford Galaxie

Ford Galaxie
Riverside 500. 1965.
Dan Gurney.

Lotus 23

Lotus 23

SECOND LEVEL OF CHANGES (FIRST BEING... →)

a) Twist key Mechanic head (left side)
slightly CCW

d) [Twist C+C (CCW) a bit More]

b) Add some 'higher poles'
LEFT and right side.

f) Push Right Again →
Twist this head
CCW, Slightly.

c) THIS STILL HAS THE
12 px BLUR ON IT →! Sort it by overlaying
originals, for new 'Merge'?

match
the C+P - cut
Top Arc to
these lines
+ straighten
flag ✓
Move this
area? Up,
down, twist?
TWIST CCW.

LOTUS

e) → Drag line to RIGHT.
LNE. 5th April 2010

Ford GT40

Nº 34 ~ 1966 Ford GT40 Mk.II. (Nº 1).

(Sorry ~ just had an idea about the
rather uninteresting 1960 Lotus 18 panel,
'Lens Flare' coming from the fuel filler cap
could liven up this otherwise drab panel.
Think of other tricks to liven up any other
'limit' panels ~ DON'T FORGET the 'Trees'
Brushes, to be used as reflections.)

+76mm
500mm
520
0 544

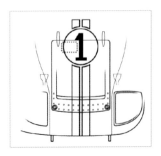

1

Lola Ford T90

№ 39 ~ 1966 Lola Ford T90 (Indy.) (Continued.) + 1967...!

Size of oval used to 'round' the far corner of №'s = W:72, H:91.

CP (Centre Point) = X: 1270 Y: 737.
Fuel Filler: Outside Diameter = 157 px's.

Gah! Blah... very hard to do!

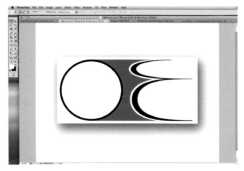

Lotus 49

Nº 45 ~ 1967 Lotus 49.

Size of individual window panes = 100 × 60 pxls. '2.6' Gaps = 20pxls. Central × 14 panes long. ∴ Window Area = 228 × (14×60 = 840 3×20 = 260) 1100 px's.

All fairly straightforward. 'Lotus' and 'Ford' ty taken from 1963 Indy cars. Lotus badge give the 'Pillow Emboss' 'Bevel & Emboss' treatment.

P.T.O For details on 'Skylights' creation.

White on Black so Filters work. ['Pixel Smear', 'Scatter', 'Diffuse Text', 'Ocean Ripple']

Original White Text.

Separate 'Text Border' Layer with 'D.Shadow', 'B&E' and...

... 'Stroke' Layer Styles.

Drop Shadow from 'Text Border' looks 'Undercut' due to Stroke.

Lotus 49B

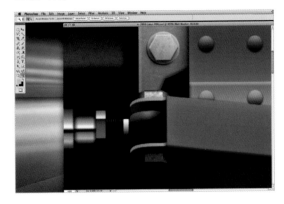

Alpine A220

Alpine

Porsche 907

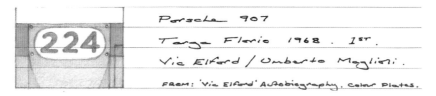

Porsche 907

Targa Florio 1968 . 1ST.

Vic Elford / Umberto Maglioli.

FROM: 'Vic Elford' Autobiography. Color Plates.

Porsche 917K – 1970

Porsche 917K.

Le Mans. 1970.

'Michael Delaney'.

(a.k.a Steve McQueen.)

Porsche 917/20 – 1971

Porsche 917/20

(a.k.a: 'The Pink Pig'; 'Big Bertha'.)

Le Mans 1971.

Reinhold Joest / Willi Kauhsen.

25·2·09 . LMR .

FROM! 'Le Mans Porsche' by John. S. Allen. LAST PAGES.

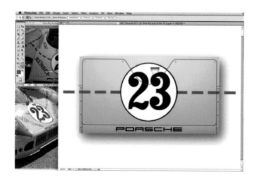

Tyrrell 006

Nº 64 ~ 1973 Tyrrell 006.

I have to say I'm pretty pleased with this Tyrrell.
Just as well given the swamp I felt like I was
crawling through during the Daytona panel, upon
my arrival here in London... But this has picked me up
and sped me back on my way. Much needed.

Brabham BT44B

Nº 65 ~ 1975 Brabham BT44.

12. September 2010, N.Mc.

There just had to be a Reutemann car! And
what better car than the BT44, one of the all-
time stunners! But... I must determine which
Grand Prix the car in the panel raced at. Find Out!
As for the Panel itself, well, the composition
HAD to be changed as my original designs (on
the iMac bore no resemblance to reality) As
far as true proportions were concerned).
That said, I am happy with the changes made.

P.T.O.

114 pxls.
194 pxls.
186 p-a.
180 pxls.
240 pxls.
320 pxls

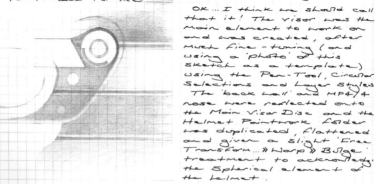

Ayrton Senna
McLaren MP4/4
Monaco GP 1988.

Sort of thing...   LMR. Mai 29. 2010

72/ McLaren MP4/4. (Ayrton Senna Helmet). I had to wait
untill returning to France to be able to work from
the 'Autosport' photo (May 13. 2010. P.23) that had
inspired this panel. So, despite my enforced
return to the UK in a couple of days for a week
here I am, and here's some necessary work,
for it and for me!

OK ... I think we should call
that it! The visor was the
main element to work on
and was created, after
much fine-tuning (and
using a 'photo' of this
sketch as a template)
using the Pen-Tool, Circular
Selections and Layer Styles.
The 'back wall' and MP4/4
nose were reflected onto
the Main Visor Disc and the
Helmet Paintwork folder
was duplicated, flattened
and given a slight 'Free
Transform... » Warp » Bulge'
treatment to acknowledge
the Spherical element of
the helmet.

As a point of note I should also... point out that
I deleted the unused 'MP4 Reflection' Folders 1-4.
I have to say, I really do like this unusual Panel!.

Ligier JS39

This drawing was to be paired with a second that showed a revised lower panel composition that I thought would help the 'Alternate Composition'. But... no!

Other ponderables include the background, the 'road', for which there are grey/mauve/sand options as well as a gradient, or not! I have also left 'strengthening' the/saturation layers in the 'Folders' containing the left and right blocks of colour. At present they are 'switched-off', but I've left them just incase.

23rd November 2010. Ken.

Toyota GT One

← 252 x 150 pxls.
← 304 x 202 pxls.
324 x 222 pxls.

(The Esso 'E' is the '3' adjusted...)

These were the dimensions initially used in making the oval 'Esso' sticker, but they have since been 'Free Transformed' (rounder), so... Download logo to be sure...

2nd December 2010, Ken.
Theo's birthday, snow.

Peugeot 908 HDi

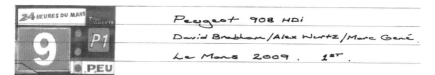

Peugeot 908 HDi
David Brabham/Alex Wurtz/Marc Gené.
Le Mans 2009.   1st.

Carbon fibre banner

DEDICATION

There are certain people who affect our lives more than they
realise. We will all remain forever indebted to Simon,
not merely because of what he taught us, but because
he provided invaluable examples of talent and dedication,
kindness, and generosity of spirit for all the people he loved.

Bon Voyage to the Driver

with love from
Paul Spicer (the co-driver)
Gus Filgate
Huw Crompton
Theo Louki
Caio Locke
Adrian Locke
Jacque Shaw

THE QUOTATIONS

At the time of my son's early death this book had not been printed. However, as far as I know, everything had been completed and was ready to go: Simon's work was done. Simon himself was thrilled that approval for **all** the quotes contained in this book had been so generously given. I am assuming this to be true, but if there is one that has slipped the net, then I am really sorry – that was not Simon's intention; nor was it mine.

David E Owen, Church Stretton, Shropshire, England